# GROW YOUR MEDITERRANEAN GARDEN
## *IN THE CITY*

ANCESTRAL WISDOM
OF THE SEAS

*Practical guide*

**VERGERS DU MONDE**

*Paying attention to them teaches us a different relationship with living beings. [Plants] show us how to notice the humble, the small, the overlooked, carving their place in the blind spots of human control.*

Marion Grange and Bronwyn Louw, *The Migrations of Plants* (Paris: Manuella Editions, 2024)

# SUMMARY

5. About Vergers du Monde
7. Nurture your ecological wisdom
8. Acknowledge and preserve
9. For whom is this guide designed?
10. Foreword
    - 11. Mediterranean legacy
    - 12. Cradle of cultures and knowledge
    - 13. A realm that bridges two realms
    - 14. Urban gardens, extraordinary havens of connection

16. **HISTORY AND EVOLUTION OF MEDITERRANEAN GARDENS**
    - 17. To the origins

21. **UNDERSTANDING THE MEDITERRANEAN ECOSYSTEM**

24. **THE FUNDAMENTALS**

28. **THE DESIGN AND LAYOUT OF YOUR GARDEN**
    - 29. Analysis and optimization of available space
    - 30. Strategizing for a year-long production journey
    - 31. Integration of traditional elements
    - 34. Embrace the beauty of natural materials
    - 35. Choose a spectrum of warm hues
    - 36. Bring shade
        - 38. The patio: history and symbolism of a central space

39. **THE URBAN MEDITERRANEAN PLANT COLLECTION**
    - 40. Iconic trees and shrubs suitable for small spaces
    - 42. Blooms and succulents for a resilient garden
    - 45. The olive tree, the vine, and the fig tree: cultivating symbols in the city

## 49. VEGETABLES AND AROMATIC PLANTS IN YOUR GARDEN
- 50. Choosing the perfect varieties for balconies and terraces
  - 53. The remarkable voyage of thyme across ages and continents
  - 55. Adequate substrates and drainage
- 56. Beneficial associations: a natural synergy
- 58. Crop rotation: a cycle of renewal
- 59. Heritage wisdom and organic fertilizers

## 64. VERTICAL CULTIVATION TO OPTIMIZE SPACE

## 68 WATER SYSTEMS
  - 69. Jmåa: where tradition meets innovation
- 70. Ancestral knowledge inspired by oases
- 74. Economical irrigation methods for your garden
  - 77. The Roman impluvium, a remarkable system for managing rainwater

## 78. GARDEN MAINTENANCE AND CARE
- 79. Specific pruning methods for Mediterranean plants
  - 81. The billhook, an emblem of Mediterranean craftsmanship
- 82. Organic pest management approaches
- 83. Attract pollinators and beneficial insects
  - 85. Bees, emblems of divinity, nobility, and wisdom
  - 86. Mediterranean beekeeping practices, a timeless tradition spanning a millennium

## 89. FROM GARDEN TO PLATE
  - 91. What embodies la dolce vita?
  - 92. Transform your Mediterranean garden into a culinary haven
- 93. Precise actions, successful harvests
- 94. Traditional preservation methods
- 99. Ancestral processing methods
  - 102. At the stone mill, the genuine creation of olive oil
- 105. Timeless recipes to embrace the bounty of your garden

## 112. IN CLOSING

## 113. A EXCLUSIVE GIFT IS WAITING JUST FOR YOU

# ABOUT VERGERS DU MONDE

*Welcome to a vibrant community where wisdom flows from near and far, uniting us in our journey to adapt to the challenges of climate change together.*

Vergers du Monde is a French organization dedicated to enhancing the ecological wisdom of farmers both locally and globally. The gatherings between local farmers and those in exile, encompassing farm visits and technical workshops, create unique opportunities for the sharing of knowledge and experiences.

In our quest for shared solutions, we aim to cultivate a realm of expression that honors this wisdom, an invaluable aspect of our intangible human heritage, providing essential insights to navigate the challenges of today.

# NURTURE YOUR ECOLOGICAL WISDOM

*Fostering a lasting connection between humanity and the natural world by sharing the wisdom of cherished traditions.*

Farming ecological knowledge embodies the timeless wisdom cultivated by countless generations of farmers. At its core lies a profound comprehension of natural cycles, seasons, and the rich tapestry of local biodiversity. These dedicated farmers have nurtured a close bond with their environment, honing their ability to perceive the delicate cues of nature that inform their agricultural endeavors.

In this profound understanding of nature, the thoughtful utilization of our natural resources stands as a vital cornerstone.

Techniques like crop rotation, water conservation, and the application of natural fertilizers stand as shining examples of this enlightened approach.

The sharing of this wisdom frequently occurs in an informal manner, through narratives, hands-on demonstrations, and active engagement in the rhythms of agricultural life.

Farming ecological wisdom holds immense significance in today's world, where sustainability and

Environmental preservation stands as a paramount concern. By weaving this understanding into contemporary agricultural practices, we can cultivate a form of agriculture that honors nature, nurturing the resilience of ecosystems and paving the way for a more sustainable agricultural future.

# ACKNOWLEDGE AND PRESERVE

*In a world of perpetual transformation, where cherished traditions face the threat of vanishing, it becomes vital to safeguard the ancestral wisdom that embodies the essence of local communities. This wisdom, lovingly passed down through the ages, transcends mere cultural legacy; it mirrors a profound bond with nature and a knowledge cultivated through patience and experience.*

*The confidentiality enveloping these practices is vital to safeguard their integrity. We are dedicated to preserving this knowledge with the highest regard, ensuring we obtain the consent of those who share it and recognizing its source. Every plant, every ritual, every remedy is anchored in a unique tradition that merits celebration in all its richness and diversity.*

*It is essential to acknowledge that these practices form a vital part of the cultural and spiritual essence of the communities that nurtured them. They are frequently shared quietly, within the intimate realm, and it is this very subtlety that safeguards their significance and worth. By honoring these traditions, we play a role in safeguarding an invaluable legacy, while celebrating the wisdom and strength of the women who tirelessly ensure their continuity.*

# FOR WHOM IS THIS GUIDE DESIGNED?

This guide is crafted for all who aspire to capture the spirit of the Mediterranean garden, even amidst the urban landscape. Whether you possess a balcony, a terrace, or a modest plot of land, this book will lead you through each step to create a sustainable, water-efficient sanctuary in perfect harmony with nature. Drawing from timeless wisdom, it is intended to empower you to nurture your own slice of the Mediterranean at home, regardless of the dimensions of your space or your gardening expertise.

*This guide is crafted for:*

- *For city dwellers who hold a deep love for nature:* those who, amidst the hustle and bustle of urban life, yearn to reconnect with the earth and cultivate a vibrant green sanctuary.
- *For enthusiasts of arid and sustainable gardens:* those eager to master the art of gardening with minimal water, employing time-honored techniques tailored for dry climates.
- *For the passionate lovers of Mediterranean flora:* those who aspire to nurture iconic plants like rosemary, olive trees, or lavender, even amidst the hustle and bustle of urban life.
- *For enthusiasts of Mediterranean culture:* those who aspire to bring the essence of Mediterranean living into their homes, through a garden that embodies the spirit of this enchanting region and its rich traditions.

# FOREWORD

Welcome to this empowering guide designed to help you cultivate your Mediterranean garden within the heart of the city, with the essential tools to transform your space into a vibrant green oasis, step by step. This guide will lead you in selecting the plants that thrive in your unique environment, teach you the art of planting, pruning, and nurturing them, while also offering aesthetic insights to embody the spirit and ambiance of the Mediterranean.

But this guide transcends the boundaries of a mere horticultural manual. We have woven in ethnocultural insights to envelop you in the timeless traditions of Mediterranean societies. We hold the conviction that sharing this wisdom, along with ancestral practices and narratives, is vital for safeguarding this vibrant heritage. You will uncover not only the art of crafting a garden inspired by the Mediterranean but also the profound cultural significance of plants and their accompanying practices.

So, you won't merely be planting a garden: you'll be nurturing a vibrant connection with traditions that transcend time and space. Prepare to enhance your living environment while rediscovering the essence of a thousand-year-old Mediterranean legacy.

# MEDITERRANEAN LEGACY

# *Cradle of cultures and knowledge*

Envision a vast azure ocean, adorned with pristine white villages nestled against towering cliffs, where the fragrant aroma of thyme and rosemary dances in the breeze. Welcome to the Mediterranean, a vibrant crossroads of civilizations that has profoundly influenced the tapestry of human history.

The Mediterranean is far more than just a sea; it stands as a magnificent bridge connecting three continents – Europe, Africa, and Asia. For millennia, it has welcomed countless peoples who have traversed its waters, leaving behind profound legacies: the Greeks, the Romans, the Phoenicians, the Arabs, the Byzantines, and the Ottomans. Each of these vibrant cultures has indelibly shaped the landscape, influenced lifestyles, and transformed the art of cultivation.

The Greeks erected magnificent temples along its shores, the Romans forged a vast maritime empire, and the Arabs brought forth exotic plants and innovative irrigation techniques that transformed Mediterranean agriculture for eternity. Each stone, each village, carries the legacy of these remarkable exchanges. The landscapes resonate with tales of the past. Centuries-old olive trees stand tall, vines embrace the hills, and gnarled fig trees tell their stories. In this realm, agriculture is not just a means of sustenance; it is a testament to resilience in the face of drought. Time-honored techniques, like mulching and the use of jars, persist as guardians of water and nurturers of the earth.

But the Mediterranean embodies a beautiful way of life. From Barcelona to Alexandria, the land is nurtured with love, and simple meals are savored, where each ingredient unfolds a tale. Olive oil, fresh herbs, and spices from the Orient create a cuisine that, beyond delight, pays homage to the earth.

Recreating a Mediterranean garden is a journey back to our roots. It is about nurturing a patch of earth, no matter how modest, in homage to these timeless cultures. It is about inviting a piece of this ancient knowledge into our lives, embracing the power to turn the small into the plentiful, to thrive in harmony with the climate while honoring the beauty of nature.

# *A realm that bridges two realms*

Beyond its ecological and aesthetic virtues, the Mediterranean garden stands as a testament to centuries of cultural exchanges and migrations. These plants, transcending borders, embody the connections between peoples and their wisdom.

Since the 19th century, the exchange between the northern and southern shores of the Mediterranean has profoundly influenced the region. People journey from one nation to another, weaving cultural connections between Europe and the Mediterranean basin. Italy, Greece, and the nations of the Levant dispatch thousands of migrants to various Mediterranean locales in pursuit of improved living conditions or fresh business ventures. These movements persist into the 20th century, especially with the migrations of Maghrebis and other communities from the southern Mediterranean basin, frequently propelled by geopolitical and economic transformations.

Colonization intensified these migratory currents, particularly during the First World War, when countless workers and soldiers from Algeria, Tunisia, and Morocco were called upon across the diverse Mediterranean landscapes. These movements, whether chosen or compelled, created profound and intricate connections among Mediterranean nations, leaving an enduring legacy in agricultural, culinary, and cultural traditions, while also establishing the groundwork for tensions stemming from inequalities and colonial exploitation.

In the vibrant 1960s, a time when France was flourishing with robust economic growth, the nation warmly welcomed a wave of immigrant workers, primarily from the Maghreb, Turkey, and Portugal. These communities, initially drawn to fulfill the demands of labor in industry and construction, ultimately found a lasting home as family reunification took root in 1976.

# *Urban gardens, extraordinary havens of connection*

This journey gives rise to a second generation that, while embracing the host society, also harbors a deep yearning to honor the traditions of their parents, especially those connected to the land and the art of agriculture.

These migrations represent more than mere movements of labor; they have fostered a vibrant exchange of knowledge, especially within the realm of agriculture. Gardens, whether nurtured by individuals or cultivated collectively, transform into sanctuaries where Mediterranean traditions thrive. Time-honored agricultural practices, such as water conservation in Mediterranean cultures, gain renewed significance as we confront today's climate challenges. These lush green spaces, frequently nestled in urban landscapes, act as cultural bridges, where plants, stories, and expertise intertwine harmoniously.

In recent times, conflicts within the Mediterranean basin, particularly the war in Syria, alongside economic crises, have sparked new waves of migration. These movements enhance European societies, especially in realms such as cuisine, music, and horticulture. Urban gardens transform into vibrant spaces of cultural exchange, where Mediterranean wisdom is reimagined, enabling migrants to nurture both their plants and their heritage.

In this noble pursuit of transmitting and preserving the rich tapestry of Mediterranean knowledge, the mission of Vergers du Monde shines brightly, as it champions these communal garden initiatives and fosters vibrant spaces for connection and exchange.

**And it is at this remarkable juncture of History that our journey intertwines with that of Omar.**

In 2023, the members of Vergers du Monde proudly secured a 100 m² plot in an urban garden, nestled within a neighborhood of a French small town. As we diligently prepared the summer seedlings, Omar, 70, approached us with a warm smile, eager to share the right techniques. Hailing from Syria, Omar expressed, *"I love it. In Syria, I had several hectares of land dedicated to gardening."*

As we delve deeper into his plot within the communal garden, we uncover vibrant rows of tomato plants, a bountiful fig tree, a pergola adorned with lush vines, and scattered patches of fragrant "nana" mint. Even though we find ourselves in the very heart of France, the gentle breeze transports us to distant lands, to the enchanting shores of Syria along the Mediterranean.

*Ready to embark on this adventure with us?*

# HISTORY AND EVOLUTION OF MEDITERRANEAN GARDENS

# TO THE ORIGINS

Mediterranean gardens are steeped in a rich history that spans millennia, tracing back to the dawn of Antiquity. As early as 3000 BC, King Gilgamesh of Mesopotamia took great pride in the lush orchards and vibrant gardens that graced the palaces and temples of his beloved city, Uruk. These early green spaces harmoniously blended utility with beauty, featuring serene interior courtyards shaded by majestic trees and illuminated by a kaleidoscope of colorful blooms.

In the heart of ancient Egypt, gardens blossomed with a blend of simplicity and brilliance. A towering wall stood guard against the relentless sands and the mighty floods of the Nile, while a carefully crafted rectangular basin secured a steady flow of life-giving water.

The trees, meticulously arranged, established a harmony that would serve as a guiding example for generations ahead.

# *Each civilization has imprinted its distinct essence on the gardens of the Mediterranean*

The Greeks introduced the notion of the sacred grove, untouched natural realms devoted to a deity or hero. They also cultivated the idea of *genius loci*, serene spots for gatherings and learning, exemplified by Plato's Academy.

*The Romans mastered the craft of the private garden, seamlessly weaving it into the fabric of domestic architecture. Within the Roman domus, the peristyle served as a sheltered gallery that flowed into an enchanting interior garden. These gardens frequently showcased frescoes illustrating the beauty of nature, crafting an illusion of boundless space.*

The Arabs brought forth the concept of the paradise garden, drawing inspiration from sacred descriptions. They celebrated vibrant colors and transformed the Mediterranean basin with a plethora of exotic plants.

# The advancement of irrigation methods has been pivotal in shaping the beauty and richness of Mediterranean gardens

The Mesopotamians crafted intricate canal systems to nourish their gardens in a challenging climate. These remarkable networks enabled them to channel water from rivers, enriching the soil and bringing life to their land.

The Romans mastered these techniques by constructing aqueducts that could carry water across vast distances. In their gardens, they incorporated fountains and basins to maintain the flow of water and elevate the beauty of their green spaces.

The Arabs, in their remarkable ingenuity, brought forth significant innovations like norias (water wheels) and qanats (underground canals), enabling the flourishing of vibrant gardens in arid landscapes.

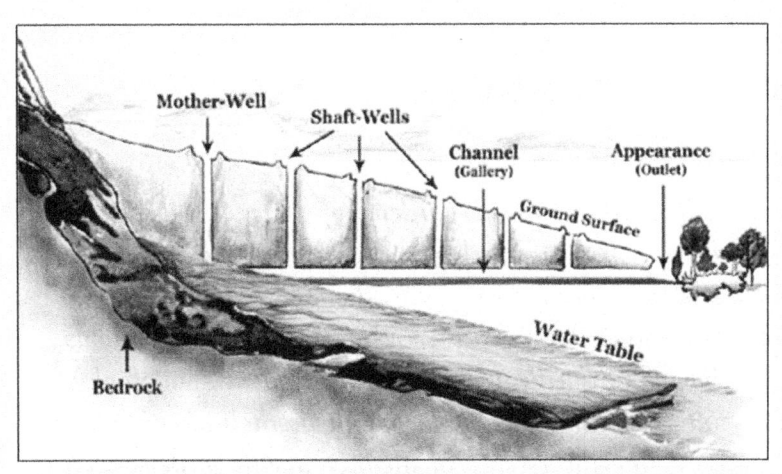

Mousazadeh, H. et al. (2023). Cultivating sustainable practices for the stewardship of underground heritage tourism: *The story of Persian qanats*.

In the ancient Mediterranean, a fascinating agricultural practice emerged known as *complant*. This technique involved the artful intercropping of diverse crops. Picture fields of cereals (ager) and vines (vitis) flourishing alongside orchards of olive, almond, or fig trees. This harmonious approach allowed for the optimization of both space and water resources, showcasing the ingenuity of our ancestors.

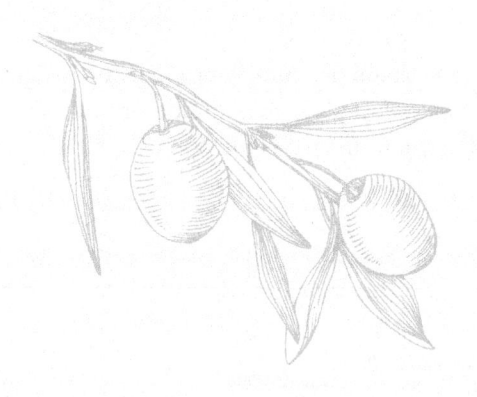

*The Mediterranean gardens of that era were not merely beautiful; they were also practical. These gardens flourished with honey plants, cereals, vegetables, and fruit trees, creating a harmonious blend of utility and elegance. This philosophy, intertwining functionality with aesthetics, continues to define the essence of Mediterranean gardens even today.*

# UNDERSTANDING THE MEDITERRANEAN ECOSYSTEM

# CLIMATE AND PLANT ADAPTATION

**Climatic attributes:**
- scorching, arid summers,
- gentle, damp winters.

**Plant adaptations:**
- leathery, small or needle-shaped leaves to reduce evapotranspiration,
- deep root systems to capture water deep down,
- summer dormancy to survive drought.

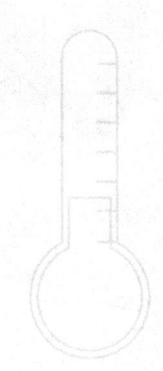

# BIODIVERSITY AND ECOLOGICAL INTERACTIONS

- The Mediterranean stands as one of the globe's 34 remarkable biodiversity hotspots.

- **Pollinators:** vital for the flourishing of plants like olive and almond trees.

- **Mycorrhizae:** empower plant roots to absorb water more effectively, particularly in times of drought.

- **Aromatic plants:** draw in helpful insects that manage pests and foster ecological harmony.

# PRESENT ENVIRONMENTAL CHALLENGES

**Climate change:**
- The Mediterranean region is experiencing a warming trend that is 20% faster than the global average.

**Heightened challenges:**
- More frequent droughts and a rise in fires.

# TRADITIONAL APPROACHES

- **Efficient irrigation:** harnessing canals and rainwater collection to optimize the use of available water.

- **Terrace cultivation:** safeguarding the soil and minimizing erosion.

- **Agroforestry:** a harmonious blend of trees and crops designed to maximize resource efficiency.

# THE FUNDAMENTALS

## 01

## BASIC PRINCIPLES

- Water conservation is essential in a Mediterranean climate, marked by scorching, arid summers. This entails selecting drought-resistant plants and employing effective irrigation methods.

- Opt for plants that embrace Mediterranean varieties or those harmonized with the local climate, resilient in the face of heat and dry spells.

- Exposure plays a pivotal role: sunlight, prevailing winds, and shaded areas must be considered to enhance plant growth and effectively manage water resources.

## 02

## ADAPTING TECHNIQUES TO SMALL SPACES

- Time-honored methods like terraced cultivation can be beautifully transformed for smaller spaces, such as using tiered planters on a balcony.

- Urban agroforestry opens the door to a world where dwarf or espalier fruit trees flourish alongside vibrant, low-growing crops.

- Traditional canal systems can be transformed into compact designs, fostering efficient irrigation solutions in limited spaces.

## 03
## CULTIVATING NURTURING MICROCLIMATES

- In the heart of the city, we have the remarkable ability to craft microclimates through the strategic use of walls, pergolas, and climbing plants, offering shade and minimizing evaporation.

- Utilizing suitable materials, like stone, can effectively manage temperature and humidity.

## 04
## SUSTAINABLE WATER MANAGEMENT

- Rainwater harvesting holds great significance in urban landscapes. Even the smallest balconies can accommodate simple systems to capture this precious resource.

- Embracing the power of mulch not only preserves the precious moisture in our soil but also lessens the frequency of our watering efforts.

## 05
## CONSERVATION OF BIODIVERSITY

- Even in modest dimensions, urban gardens can significantly contribute to the preservation of Mediterranean biodiversity.

- Selecting native flora and establishing diverse environments (arid zones, water sources) can draw an array of wildlife.

# THE DESIGN AND LAYOUT OF YOUR GARDEN

# 01

## ANALYSIS AND OPTIMIZATION OF AVAILABLE SPACE

- Evaluate the sunlight exposure in your area (balcony, terrace, small garden).

- Recognize the spaces of shade and sunlight that dance across the day.

- Consider the challenges of urban life, such as wind, pollution, and the constraints of limited space.

- Embrace verticality: living walls, climbing vines, and elevated shelves.

- Enhance every space: living room zones, dining zones, cultivation zones.

## 02

## STRATEGIZING FOR A YEAR-LONG PRODUCTION JOURNEY

- Select plants that bloom or produce in a staggered manner.

- Unite annuals, perennials, and shrubs to create a tapestry of beauty that captivates throughout the seasons.

- Incorporate fragrant herbs for ongoing abundance.

- Design rotations for container vegetable gardens.

- Create a sanctuary for both summer and winter blooms.

## 03

# INTEGRATION OF TRADITIONAL ELEMENTS

❋ Craft a sanctuary of shade and strength for your climbing plants with a beautifully designed **pergola**.

❋ Infuse your space with a genuine essence by incorporating **terracotta jars and pottery** that also function as beautiful containers.

❋ Craft delicate **dry stone walls** to define spaces or construct charming planters.

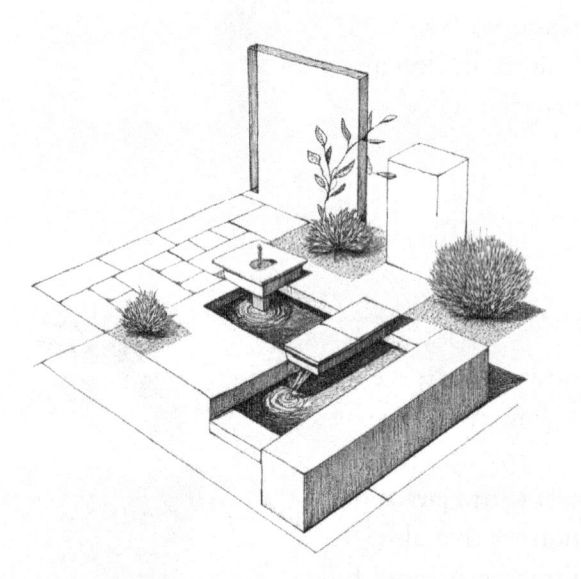

❋ Infuse your space with a refreshing essence and a gentle symphony of sound through the enchanting presence of **fountains or charming water features**.

❋ Lay down **gravel or natural stone pathways** to beautifully define the garden space.

❋ Design a quintessential Mediterranean oasis for relaxation, featuring a charming **stone or wooden bench**.

## 04

# EMBRACE THE BEAUTY OF NATURAL MATERIALS

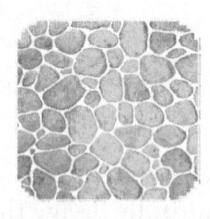

- ROCK
- OLIVE WOOD
- CYPRESS WOOD
- TERRA COTTA

## 05

# CHOOSE A SPECTRUM OF WARM HUES

✻ Ochres, terracottas, whites, beiges, Mediterranean blue

## 06

## BRING SHADE

*Shade is an essential element in a Mediterranean garden, alleviating water stress on plants and minimizing evaporation. It transforms outdoor spaces into inviting areas for relaxation and dining. Furthermore, it fosters a balanced microclimate by moderating temperatures, offering a cooler and more harmonious atmosphere for both plant vitality and human enjoyment.*

### VARIETIES OF TREES FOR SHADE

- **The olive tree**: with its lush foliage, offers a gentle shade, perfectly adapted to thrive in warm climates.
- **Fig tree**: a timeless Mediterranean marvel that offers abundant shade.
- **Albizia**: celebrated for its delicate leaves and ornamental charm, it offers a delightful refuge from the sun.

### ORGANIC DRAPES

- **Bamboo or reed screens**: eco-friendly, biodegradable sails that offer shade while preserving the purity of our environment.

- **Lush canopies**: embrace climbing plants such as vines or jasmine to create natural shade in your spaces, all while avoiding artificial materials.

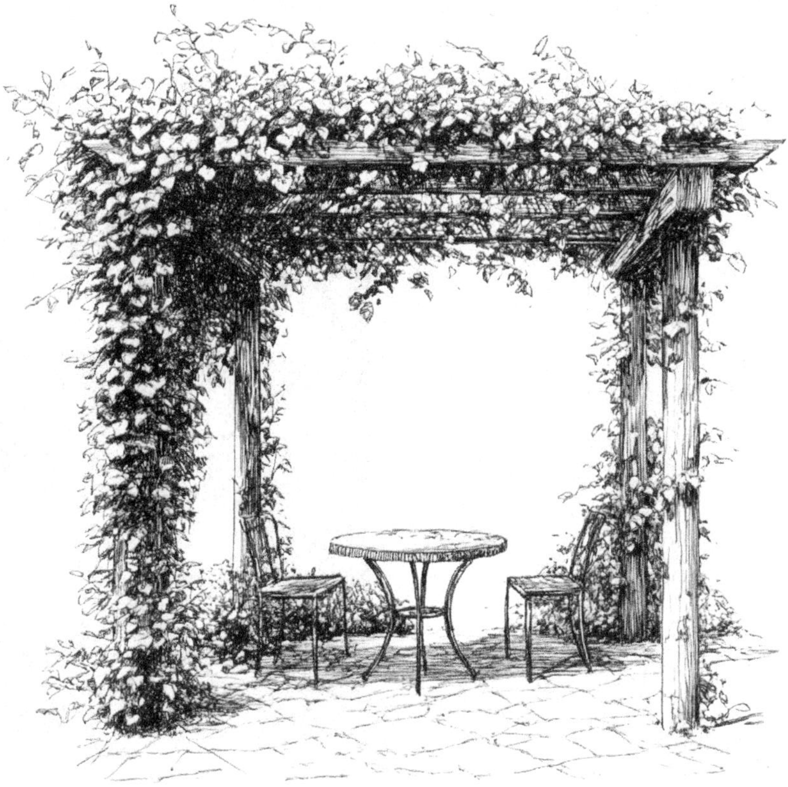

# *The patio: history and symbolism of a central space*

*The patio transcends the notion of a mere architectural space; it captures the soul of Mediterranean homes. Emerging from the grandeur of Roman architecture, this open-air interior garden, typically embraced by galleries, has evolved into a cherished symbol through the ages. Enriched by the influences of Christian and Islamic cultures, the Hispano-Moorish Andalusian patio stands as a remarkable testament. This serene microclimate, often adorned with a fountain, not only refreshes the home but also embodies the spirit of intimacy, hospitality, and togetherness.*

The idea of the patio traces back to the homes of the Romans and Greco-Romans, where these areas were envisioned as the very essence of life. In time, Islamic architecture, particularly in the Iberian Peninsula, enhanced this legacy. The Andalusian patio, emerging from the Arab influence in Spain, journeyed alongside colonists to Hispanic America. Each culture infused its unique perspective while honoring the significance of a sheltered and nurturing space, devoted to reflection and rejuvenation.

In the heart of traditional Mediterranean homes lies the patio, a sanctuary that embraces light in spaces often devoid of exterior windows. It serves as a vital element in navigating the warmth of hot climates, with its oasis-like design fostering a tranquil microclimate. Beyond being a mere resting place, the patio embodies the spirit of sharing, hospitality, and a retreat from the sweltering heat, creating an intimate haven for cherished moments with family and friends.

# THE URBAN MEDITERRANEAN PLANT COLLECTION

## 01

# ICONIC TREES AND SHRUBS SUITABLE FOR SMALL SPACES

### DWARF OLIVE TREE OR ESPALIER

- **Latin name:** Olea europaea
- **Planting season:** March to May
- **Care:** gentle trimming post-bloom, balanced hydration
- **Soil type:** well-drained, arid to gently chalky soil

### CYPRESS OF PROVENCE IN COLUMN

- **Latin name:** Cupressus sempervirens
- **Planting season:** October through March
- **Care:** gentle trimming, balanced hydration
- **Soil type:** well-drained, light soil, embraces limestone

### OLEANDER COMPACT

- **Latin name:** Nerium oleander
- **Planting season:** April to June
- **Care:** gentle trimming post-bloom, consistent hydration during dry spells
- **Soil type:** well-draining earth, resilient in less fertile conditions

### DWARF PITTOSPORUM

- **Latin name:** Pittosporum tobira 'Nana'
- **Planting season:** March to May
- **Care:** gentle trimming to preserve form, hydration
- **Soil type:** well-drained, gently acidic to neutral soil

# 02

# BLOOMS AND SUCCULENTS FOR A RESILIENT GARDEN

### LAVENDER

- **Latin name**: Lavandula angustifolia
- **Planting season:** March to May
- **Care**: yearly trimming post-bloom, gentle watering
- **Soil type:** well-drained, nutrient-deficient, calcareous soil

### AGAPANTHUS

- **Latin name:** Agapanthus africanus
- **Planting season:** October to March
- **Care:** trim stems post-bloom, ensure moderate watering during dry spells
- **Soil type:** well-drained, nutrient-rich, slightly acidic to neutral soil

### *SANTOLINA*

- **Latin name:** Santolina chamaecyparissus
- **Planting season:** April to May
- **Care:** gentle trimming post-bloom, balanced hydration
- **Soil type:** arid, well-drained, nutrient-deficient soil

### *AGAVES*

- **Latin name:** Agave americana
- **Planting season:** April to June
- **Care:** minimal water needs, trimming of dead leaves
- **Soil type:** light, arid, nutrient-deficient soil

## *EUPHORBIAS*

- **Latin name:** Euphorbia spp.
- **Planting season:** March to May
- **Care:** minimal care required, trimming post-bloom, gentle watering
- **Soil type:** well-drained, arid to calcareous earth

## *CISTUS*

- **Latin name:** Cistus
- **Planting season:** April to June
- **Care:** trimming after blooming, balanced hydration
- **Soil type:** dry, calcareous soil that is well-drained

# 03

# THE OLIVE TREE, THE VINE, AND THE FIG TREE: CULTIVATING SYMBOLS IN THE CITY

## *SELECTION OF OLIVE VARIETIES*

- **Arbequina**: a compact marvel, bearing fruit abundantly throughout.
- **Picholine**: resilient to the chill
- **Cypress**: towering forms

## *PRUNING*

- **Spring**: clear away the lifeless branches
- **Summer**: remove new shoots
- **Winter**: trim to preserve form

## *GROWING IN POTS*

- Container with a minimum diameter of 50 cm
- Soil that allows for proper drainage
- **Watering**: Once or twice a week during the summer season.
- **Exposure**: directly south

## SELECTION OF GRAPE VARIETIES

- **Hamburg Muscat:** exquisite table grapes
- **Golden Chasselas:** vibrant, fruitful

## SETUP AND PRUNING

- **In a pot:** minimum 40 cm diameter
- **On a trellis:** attach horizontal wires
- **Winter:** cut back to 2-3 buds
- **Summer:** pinch back overly long shoots

## CARE

- Regular watering in summer
- Winter protection if necessary
- Thinning of grape clusters
- Leaf removal to promote ripening

## SELECTION OF FIG TREE VARIETIES

- **Brown Turkey:** resilient, compact, and able to withstand the chill
- **Ronde de Bordeaux:** a perfect choice for compact areas, offering an early start.
- **Madeleine of the Two Seasons**: abundant, yielding two harvests each year

## CARE

- **Planting**: basking in full sunlight, thriving in well-drained soil
- **Watering**: consistent in the first year, then balanced
- **Pruning**: a gentle touch in spring to preserve beauty.

## CAUTION POINT

- Vulnerable to intense frost (below -10°C)
- May encounter fig fly in warmer climates

**There are constants.**

Wherever the Vergers du Monde team has ventured, on the fringes of the bustling Parisian metropolises, where immigrant communities have made their homes since the 1980s and where urban gardens have thrived amidst the apartment blocks, Mediterranean individuals consistently nurture a fig tree, which thrives beautifully, alongside vines, often gracefully entwined around a handcrafted pergola.

Omar, whom we introduced at the outset of this guide, embodies this sentiment perfectly. He revealed to us the profound connection these two plants have with his village, his homeland, and the fragrant memories they conjure.

# VEGETABLES AND AROMATIC PLANTS IN YOUR GARDEN

## 01

# CHOOSING THE PERFECT VARIETIES FOR BALCONIES AND TERRACES

### *CHERRY TOMATOES*

- **Varieties:** Sweetie, Balconi Red
- **Sowing:** March-April
- **Planting:** May-June

### *MINIATURE PEPPERS*

- **Varieties:** Miniature Cocoa, Little Marseillais
- **Sowing:** February-March
- **Planting:** May

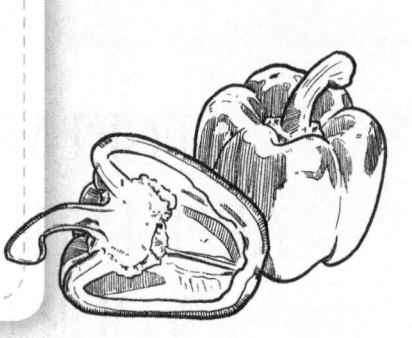

### *MINIATURE EGGPLANTS*

- **Varieties:** Patio Baby, Hansel
- **Sowing:** March
- **Planting:** May-June

### *COMPACT ZUCCHINI*

- **Varieties:** Patio Star, Buckingham
- **Sowing:** April-May
- **Planting:** May-June

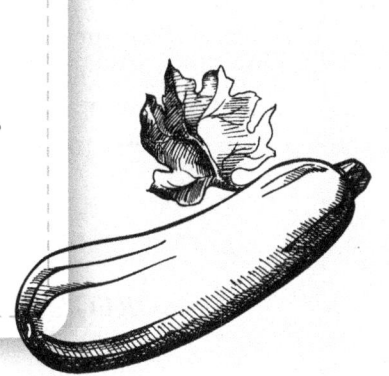

# HERBS

### ROSEMARY
- Rosmarinus officinalis
- **Planting:** spring or autumn

### THYME
- Thymus vulgaris
- **Planting:** spring or autumn

### BASIL
- Ocimum basilicum
- **Planting:** May-June

### OREGANO
- Origanum vulgare
- **Planting:** April-May

# *The remarkable voyage of thyme across ages and continents*

*Thyme, with its rich heritage in the Mediterranean basin, has traversed the ages, embraced by cultures that have cherished it for its fragrant and healing properties.*

Since the dawn of ancient Egypt (3000 BC), it has played a vital role in funeral rituals, while in Greece, it stands as a symbol of courage. Throughout the Middle Ages, it became an essential ingredient in love potions crafted by "witches" and was discreetly placed under pillows to banish nightmares. During the Renaissance, it flourished in the medicinal gardens of monasteries, and in 17th century England, it was employed to alleviate epilepsy and headaches. In the 18th century, it made its way to North America through the hands of colonists. European settlers embraced it as a favored remedy for colds. Today, it flourishes across the globe, thriving in diverse and arid climates, all the while honoring its Mediterranean roots. Whether gracing our dishes as *Herbes de Provence* or enriching our lives through aromatherapy, its legacy persists, deeply woven into the fabric of cultural and medical traditions worldwide.

## MINT

- Mint spicata *Nanah*

## CULTIVATION

- **Planting**: during spring, starting in March
- Cultivate soil that is thoughtfully enriched with organic matter.
- Position plants in space with a minimum distance of 40 cm between them
- You can effortlessly multiply it through stem cuttings or by dividing clumps.

## LIMIT ITS INVASIVE NATURE

- Place it in pots or containers, even if you choose to partially immerse them in the earth.
- Establish a resilient rhizome barrier using tiles or boards firmly anchored into the earth.
- Regularly trim the plant to guide its growth.

## 02

# ADEQUATE SUBSTRATES AND DRAINAGE

**HERBS**

- **Blend:** 60% potting soil + 30% sand + 10% compost
- **pH:** 6,5 - 7,5
- **Drainage:** a layer of 2-3 cm of gravel or clay balls at the base of the pot

**SHRUBS**

- **Blend:** 50% potting soil + 30% garden soil + 20% coarse sand
- **pH:** 6,5 - 8,0
- **Drainage:** a layer of 3-4 cm of gravel at the base of the pot

**POTTED TREES**

- **Blend:** 40% potting soil + 30% garden soil + 20% compost + 10% perlite
- **pH:** 6,5 - 8,5
- **Drainage:** a layer of 5 cm of gravel or fragments of broken pots at the base

**PLANTS SUCCULENTS**

- **Blend:** 50% unique cactus soil + 50% gritty sand or pozzolan
- **pH:** 6,0 - 7,5
- **Drainage:** a layer of 3-4 cm of fine gravel resting at the base of the pot.

# 03

# BENEFICIAL ASSOCIATIONS: A NATURAL SYNERGY

*Combining plants fosters a harmonious alliance that nurtures their growth while warding off unwanted pests.*

### TOMATOES + BASIL
Basil wards off pests while elevating the taste of tomatoes. When these two crops are planted side by side, they cultivate a beautiful synergy in the vegetable garden.

### PEPPER + OREGANO
Oregano elevates the taste of peppers and plays a role in safeguarding against certain diseases.

## CABBAGE + THYME

Thyme repels cabbage worm and its strong odor disorients the pests.

## CARROT + ROSEMARY

Rosemary keeps the carrot fly away, while improving the flavor of the carrots.

## 04

# CROP ROTATION: A CYCLE OF RENEWAL

*Crop rotation preserves the health of the soil, preventing its depletion and ensuring a better harvest each season.*

### LEAVES + FRUITS + TUBERS

Rotating these categories nurtures soil vitality and safeguards against nutrient exhaustion.

### LETTUCE + TOMATO + CARROT

Lettuce enhances the soil with nitrogen, nurturing the growth of tomatoes, while carrots create pathways in the earth, preparing it for future harvests.

## 05

# HERITAGE WISDOM AND ORGANIC FERTILIZERS

### OLIVE POMACE

*Olive pomace is the remarkable solid byproduct that emerges after the extraction of olive oil. It is primarily composed of the skin, fragments of pulp, pits, and occasionally a trace of residual oil.*

Abundant in essential nutrients, particularly potassium, they serve as a remarkable natural fertilizer. When converted into compost, they enrich the soil profoundly, preventing nitrogen depletion and fostering vibrant growth.

**Caution: use with moderation to prevent an overload of potassium and space out applications to promote optimal absorption.**

# WOOD ASHES

*Wood ashes, abundant in potassium, calcium, and essential trace elements, serve as a remarkable enhancement for acidic soils. They play a vital role in balancing the soil's pH, yet their application should be approached with care.*

**Ways to utilize them:**

- Ideal around fruit trees.
- Apply 150 g/m$^2$ to neutral or acidic soil.
- **Precautions**: avoid them on already alkaline soils or for acidophilic plants, and do not exceed 250 g/m$^2$ per year to maintain a good balance.

# SEAWEED

*For centuries, seaweed has been a cherished ally in enriching the soil along the Mediterranean and Atlantic coasts. Its remarkable contributions are celebrated for their abundance of trace elements, such as copper and manganese, as well as potassium, all while enhancing the very structure of the earth beneath our feet.*

Before utilizing them, it is crucial to purify the seaweed by allowing it to bask in the elements for several weeks. Once prepared, it can serve as mulch or be blended into the soil, frequently alongside compost. This organic matter enriches your garden in a sustainable manner.

Seaweed enhances soil structure, enriching its fertility. It also establishes a natural barrier against specific pests, while promoting improved moisture retention.

# MANURE FROM GOATS AND SHEEP

*Goat and sheep manure are treasures in the world of agriculture, celebrated for their abundant nutrients, especially nitrogen and potassium, which are vital for thriving crops. Sheep manure shines brightly for flowering and fruiting vegetables, owing to its impressive potash content.*

These fertilizers enhance the soil's structure, boosting its porosity and ability to retain water, a vital factor in Mediterranean areas where the earth frequently faces dryness and unpredictable rainfall.

For centuries, goat and sheep manure has played a vital role in Mediterranean agriculture, serving as a powerful organic amendment that enriches the soil with essential organic matter and fosters vibrant microbial life. To maximize its benefits and prevent nutrient overload, it is advisable to compost these manures thoroughly before application, ensuring optimal absorption by plants.

# TRANSFORMING OLIVE BRANCHES INTO A NURTURING MULCH

*This technique has its roots in the ancient Mediterranean, where the care of olive groves holds great significance. Shredding branches after pruning serves not only to recycle waste but also to enrich the soil. Historically, this practice emerged as a safer alternative to burning, a method that posed risks in these arid landscapes.*

By transforming olive branches into mulch after pruning, we cultivate a blend rich in organic matter that fortifies the soil structure and enhances moisture retention. This approach not only recycles waste on-site but also presents a sustainable solution for our environment.

Embracing the Mediterranean climate, where each precious drop of water holds immense value, this practice embodies a time-honored approach to stewardship that honors the environment, exemplified by the incorporation of aromatic plants and mineral mulch in the enchanting gardens of the Mediterranean.

# VERTICAL CULTIVATION TO OPTIMIZE SPACE

*Crafting a vertical herb garden in the city is a brilliant way to make the most of limited space while infusing urban life with lush greenery and fresh herbs. This method enables you to utilize walls, balconies, or small nooks, turning every inch into a thriving ecosystem. By merging beauty with functionality, this system creates a natural oasis in the city, fostering food independence and a direct bond with nature, even in the tightest of spaces.*

## 01

## USE OF RECYCLED PALLETS

- Prepare and smooth the palette.
- Incorporate a plywood base to support the soil.
- Craft sections using horizontal panels.
- Line the interior with geotextile to preserve moisture.
- Fill with potting soil designed for fragrant plants.

## 02
## POCKET GROWING SYSTEMS

- Utilize felt or geotextile pockets.
- Secure them to a vertical support (wall, wire mesh).
- Select bags of various sizes based on the plants.
- Fill with radiant, well-draining potting soil.

## 03
## AUTOMATED IRRIGATION FOR GREEN WALL

- Set up a drip irrigation system.
- Position the drippers over each pocket or compartment.
- Link to a timer for consistent watering.
- Install a water collection tray at the base of the wall.

## 04

# ADDITIONAL ADVICE

- Select plants that thrive in vertical gardens, such as thyme, rosemary, oregano, and basil.

- Position the most drought-resistant plants at the highest point.

- Embrace the warmth of the sun, allowing its golden rays to grace your life for at least 6 hours each day.

- Nourish your plants consistently with a liquid organic fertilizer.

# WATER SYSTEMS

# *Jmåa: where tradition meets innovation*

*In every corner of the globe, water has consistently emerged as a vital force, shaping the very fabric of social and economic structures. Beyond being merely a resource, it embodies the essence of survival and strength. The fair stewardship of this precious element is crucial for fostering the well-being of our communities. From age-old practices like the jmåa to the modern urban gardens of today, water stands as a fundamental cornerstone of humanity, demanding our careful and sustainable attention.*

*The jmåa stands as a testament to the wisdom of ancestral community institutions in the rural Mediterranean, particularly within the serene palm groves. It embodies the principles of collective and equitable stewardship of water, a vital resource in these arid landscapes. Guided by an amin, a seasoned individual chosen for their expertise, the jmåa establishes the customary rules known as izerfan n'ouaman, which govern the intricate dance of irrigation. This remarkable framework facilitates the fair distribution of water rights among families, regulates the cycles of irrigation, and orchestrates water turns, ensuring that this precious resource is utilized sustainably and justly. Beyond its practical implications, this system resonates with profound social and symbolic significance. Water management transforms into a collective act of unity, fortifying the bonds among community members while nurturing a delicate harmony with the environment.*

*In one of the urban gardens we explored, lovingly tended by Mediterranean families for many decades, water is overseen by the city, with each plot allotted a predetermined quota, irrespective of the unique needs of the crops. During periods of drought, when restrictions tighten, gardeners steadfastly uphold the essence of their traditions. In an informal yet resourceful manner, they reconfigure the distribution of water, maximizing its use to be more efficient and to better cater to the diverse needs of the plants they nurture.*

## 01

# ANCESTRAL KNOWLEDGE INSPIRED BY OASES

## THE FOGGARAS

*Foggaras represent a vital legacy of irrigation in the oases, especially in Algeria. This intricate network of subterranean galleries, crafted over centuries, harnesses water from elevated groundwater sources and gracefully channels it by gravity to the fields that flourish under its care.*

This ancient system plays a vital role in reducing evaporation in the arid landscapes of the Algerian Sahara. Yet, this invaluable ecosystem now faces challenges from the impacts of climate change and the slow decline of this traditional practice.

*If the foggaras vanish, numerous oases may wither, resulting in profound ecological, economic, and social repercussions.*

# THE SEGUIAS

*Originating primarily from North Africa, especially the Saharan and Maghreb regions, seguias are remarkable open-air irrigation channels, carved into the earth or fortified with materials like stone or concrete.*

These canals meander through the oases, transporting water from a source, typically a river or aquifer, to nourish the crops. They function on the principle of equitable water sharing, where each farmer is allocated a designated irrigation period, often measured by traditional indicators like hourglasses or shadows. This carefully timed distribution system guarantees a just allocation, customized to meet the needs of the crops.

# THE GHOUT TECHNIQUE

*The ghout technique is a time-honored irrigation method that has flourished in the El Oued region of Algeria since the 15th century.*

This method encompasses the excavation of a crater ranging from 80 to 200 meters in diameter and approximately 10 meters deep within the sand dunes, enabling the roots of the date palms to access the water table directly. The water ascends through capillarity, thereby removing the necessity for surface irrigation. Tailored to thrive in the desert climate, this approach nurtures biodiversity and safeguards against silting.

However, it faces a perilous challenge from the advent of modern techniques like deep drilling and pivot irrigation, which could result in its vanishing.

## 02

# ECONOMICAL IRRIGATION METHODS FOR YOUR GARDEN

### *IRRIGATION NETWORK*

- **Principle:** inspired by localized irrigation, this system brings water directly to the roots of plants, thus minimizing losses by evaporation.

- **Urban adaptation:** implement drip irrigation systems in planters or on balconies for efficient and water-conserving watering.

### *MINI-CHANNELS OR FURROWS*

- Drawing inspiration from the seguias system, craft a miniature network of channels utilizing gutters, halved PVC pipes, or elongated trays.
- Position these mini-channels on a gentle incline to enable water to cascade effortlessly by the force of gravity.
- Link them to your rainwater collection system.
- Incorporate small valves or removable plugs to masterfully regulate the flow of water to various sections of your garden.
- Utilize porous materials or create openings along the channels to facilitate a gentle, ongoing flow of irrigation.

## THE ART OF CAPTURING RAINWATER

- Set up rainwater collectors linked to the gutters of your roof or balcony.
- Select tanks that are appropriately sized to complement your space, ranging from 100 to 1000 liters based on the available surface area.
- Incorporate a straightforward filtration system to eliminate debris.
- Link the tank to your mini-channel network or drip system.
- Embrace the power of a solar pump to enhance the flow of water distribution when the need arises.
- Incorporate decorative reservoirs or seamlessly blend them into the design of your space (for example: planters with built-in reservoirs).

# *The Roman impluvium, a remarkable system for managing rainwater*

*The impluvium, a symbol of Roman ingenuity, stands as a testament to exceptional water management in the Mediterranean, where every drop is invaluable. This remarkable rainwater collection system features a central basin, often nestled in the heart of the atrium, crafted to gather water cascading through an opening in the roof known as a compluvium. The collected water was meticulously filtered and channeled to an underground cistern for enduring storage. This system transcended mere functionality; it also contributed to cooling the interiors of homes, while serving as a stunning focal point, embodying the harmonious blend of utility and beauty in Roman architecture.*

Over the years, the impluvium transformed to signify not just this central basin, but the entire system for collecting rainwater, encompassing the catchment area, the transport network, and the storage facilities. These cisterns and pipes embodied a sustainable solution, foreshadowing modern practices in today's Mediterranean urban landscapes. The significance of these traditional methods extends beyond their technical brilliance; it also encompasses their social aspect: as water is central to the fabric of daily life, it mirrors the collective practices of supply and exchange that endure in certain rural communities.

# GARDEN MAINTENANCE AND CARE

## SPECIFIC PRUNING METHODS FOR MEDITERRANEAN PLANTS

- **Climate adaptation:** Mediterranean plants are generally adapted to hot and dry conditions. Light pruning is often enough to maintain their shape and promote good air circulation, which helps prevent disease.

- **Timing: pruning** should take place after the flowering period for plants like lavender, encouraging fresh growth while maintaining the beauty of the blossoms.

### SANTOLINA

Gently trim after the blossoms fade, during the summer months.

Trim down to create a more streamlined form.

Prune more rigorously every 3-4 years to revitalize the plant.

### ROSEMARY

Gently prune in the spring, right after the blossoms have appeared.

Trim the branches by approximately 2-3 cm to encourage fresh growth.

Steer clear of slicing into aged timber, for it does not regenerate with ease.

### OLIVIE TREE

Prune during the late winter or early spring, just before the vibrant growth begins anew.

Eliminate branches that are dead, diseased, or crossing each other.

Prune the center of the tree to enhance air circulation and allow light to filter through.

# *The billhook, an emblem of Mediterranean craftsmanship*

*The billhook, distinguished by its signature curved blade, stands as a vital emblem of the agricultural legacy in the Mediterranean regions. Crafted from metal, it has been a trusted tool for pruning olive trees, grapevines, and various fruit trees, enhancing the aeration of the plants and elevating their productivity.*

Its design enables meticulous cutting, minimizing harm to plants and promoting their recovery. Handed down through the ages, the billhook embodies artisanal and sustainable craftsmanship, showcasing reverence for natural rhythms and the local landscape. Traditionally, it is linked to eco-friendly agricultural methods, where farmers harness local resources while honoring the surrounding ecosystem.

The billhook's origins are shrouded in mystery, making it challenging to pinpoint a specific country of origin. This remarkable agricultural tool has been utilized for centuries across various Mediterranean regions and beyond. Its roots likely trace back to antiquity, flourishing in the civilizations of ancient Greece and Rome. Over time, its influence expanded to other Mediterranean nations, including Spain, Italy, and southern France, where it emerged as an essential component of cherished agricultural traditions.

# 02

# ORGANIC PEST MANAGEMENT APPROACHES

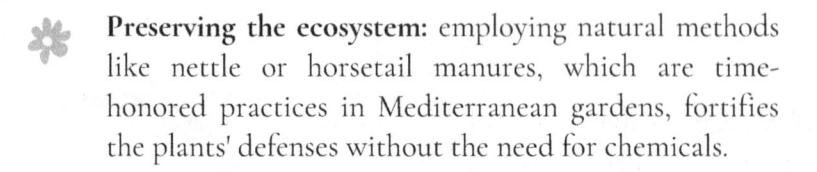

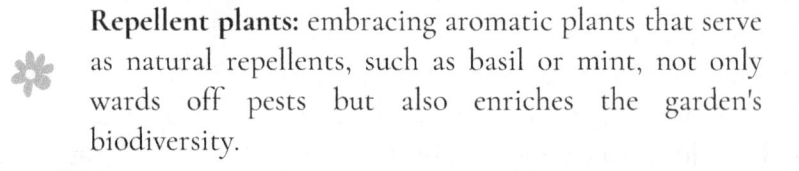

- **Preserving the ecosystem:** employing natural methods like nettle or horsetail manures, which are time-honored practices in Mediterranean gardens, fortifies the plants' defenses without the need for chemicals.

- **Repellent plants:** embracing aromatic plants that serve as natural repellents, such as basil or mint, not only wards off pests but also enriches the garden's biodiversity.

- **Effective irrigation systems:** drip irrigation, designed to minimize moisture on leaves, can significantly lower the occurrence of fungal diseases and draw fewer insect pests.

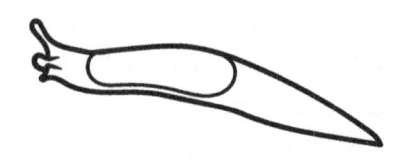

## 03

# ATTRACT POLLINATORS AND BENEFICIAL INSECTS

- Cultivating **fragrant herbs like thyme, rosemary, lavender, and sage** is a time-honored tradition that effortlessly draws in a multitude of pollinators. These remarkable plants thrive in the Mediterranean climate, flourishing with minimal water needs.

- Constructing **dry stone walls** is an age-old craft that offers refuge to countless beneficial insects and pollinators. The gaps between the stones create havens and nesting grounds.

- Preserving **patches of *garrigue* or scrubland adjacent to crops** is a time-honored tradition that fosters biodiversity and draws in pollinators.

🌼 **Terrace cultivation**, a time-honored practice, fosters microclimates that are welcoming to pollinators and beneficial insects, offering a rich tapestry of habitats and floral resources.

🌼 Mediterranean farmers have long embraced **local varieties of fruit trees and vegetables**, which are often more harmoniously aligned with the needs of local pollinators.

🌼 In the arid embrace of the Mediterranean climate, the art of **crafting small water features**—such as ponds and fountains—stands as a cherished tradition, drawing in pollinators and beneficial allies.

🌼 An age-old tradition, **crop rotation**, frequently incorporating legumes, fosters a rich tapestry of floral diversity and draws an array of pollinators throughout the seasons.

# *Bees, emblems of divinity, nobility, and wisdom*

*Bees held a pivotal role in the heart of Mediterranean cultures, embodying both symbolic and spiritual significance. In ancient Greece, they were revered as divine messengers selected by Zeus, representing purity and wisdom. They were also associated with great intellectuals, like Plato, who, according to legends, experienced a touch from bees in his youth, heralding the brilliance that would define his future.*

In ancient Egypt, bees held a sacred place, symbolizing the Pharaoh's power and his bond with the divine. The products of these remarkable creatures, honey and wax, played a vital role in funerary traditions: honey served as offerings to the gods, while wax was integral to the mummification process and the creation of sacred art.

Honey, revered as a symbol of life and prosperity, played a significant role in numerous birth and marriage ceremonies throughout the Mediterranean region. Mead, a delightful alcoholic drink crafted from honey, was hailed as "the nectar of the gods," highlighting the profound spiritual significance of bees in these ancient cultures.

# *Mediterranean beekeeping practices, a timeless tradition spanning a millennium*

Traditional beekeeping practices in the Mediterranean region showcase remarkable ingenuity in adapting to local resources and conditions. The types of hives are diverse, featuring ceramic hives in areas like North Africa, cylindrical cork hives in various Mediterranean locales, and basketwork hives in northern France. These time-honored methods trace their roots back to ancient Egypt (2400 BCE), where the use of ceramic cylinders first emerged, eventually spreading across the Mediterranean basin.

The earliest archaeological evidence of beekeeping emerges from this remarkable period, with depictions discovered in the sun temple of Abu Gorab, showcasing advanced bee management techniques. In Greece, as early as the 5th century BCE, and in Spain during the 3rd century, the innovative use of ceramic hives became a method for harvesting honey. The wisdom of beekeeping then traversed the ages, lovingly passed down through generations with little alteration. Yet, honey harvesting in ancient times posed significant challenges: lacking removable combs, which were only developed in the 19th century, beekeepers often faced the difficult task of partially or entirely dismantling colonies to retrieve the honey. It was only through the passage of time that groundbreaking innovations emerged, allowing for a reduction in these losses.

Archaeological evidence of these hives is scarce, as the materials employed, including straw, wicker, and wood, are prone to decay. Yet, the remarkable discovery in 2007 of thirty raw earth hives, dating back to 900 BCE in Tel Rehov, Israel, highlights the significance of beekeeping in this region for millennia. This ancient expertise, intertwined with honey collection and hive stewardship, showcases the resilience of Mediterranean communities and their deep-rooted connection to this vital practice, which is crucial for both the economy and local heritage.

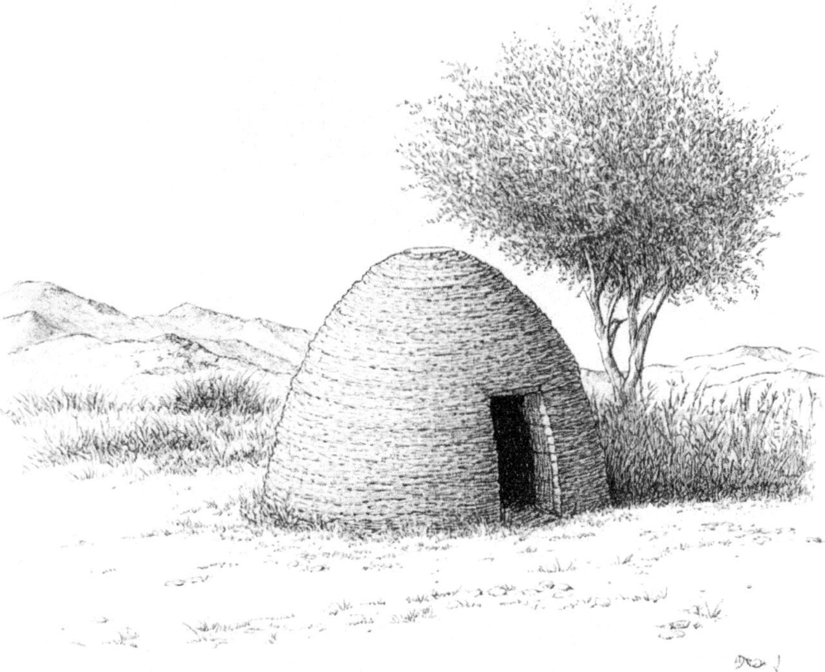

*Is your garden under siege by pests, and are you seeking a natural and effective solution to reclaim it? Uncover our practical guide, Protect Your Garden Without Chemicals: Mauritian Ancestral Knowledge.*

*Crafted in partnership with a gardener of Mauritian heritage, this guide brims with invaluable wisdom handed down through the ages. Within its pages, you will discover time-honored, straightforward, and eco-conscious methods to safeguard your plants while embracing the beauty of nature.*

*Unite your wisdom and unveil these time-tested solutions!*

# FROM GARDEN TO PLATE

*That's it, your garden is now bursting with vitality!*

From concept to creation, there lies but a single step. Amidst the vibrant chaos of the city, the blaring horns, and the relentless rhythm of life, this serene green oasis whisks you away: to a getaway, to the coast, in a space that embodies health, elegance, beauty, and grace, where time-honored traditions harmonize with modern advancements to present you with the finest. Your Mediterranean garden awaits.

# What embodies la dolce vita?

*La dolce vita embodies the spirit of the Mediterranean way of life, a tribute to beauty and the joy found in simple pleasures. Embracing this philosophy in your urban Mediterranean garden transforms it into a sanctuary of harmony and well-being. Each nook becomes a haven for relaxation and connection, adorned with fragrant plants that awaken the senses and natural elements that beckon tranquility.*

The essence of la dolce vita emerged in post-war Italy during the vibrant 1950s and 1960s, a time characterized by economic prosperity known as the "Italian economic miracle." This era fostered a newfound appreciation for life's simple joys and the warmth of togetherness. Immortalized by Federico Fellini's 1960 masterpiece La Dolce Vita, the term has come to symbolize a way of living that embraces pleasure, simplicity, and the exquisite art of cherishing every moment.

In your urban Mediterranean garden, discover the ways to weave this beautiful art of living into your space:

- **Aesthetics:** cultivate a serene environment by incorporating plants and embracing the beauty of natural materials such as stone and wood.

- **Relaxation:** create inviting spaces to unwind or enjoy a meal in the great outdoors.

- **Mediterranean cuisine:** harness the bounty of your vegetable garden, fruit trees, and herbs to create nourishing and wholesome meals.

# *Transform your Mediterranean garden into a culinary haven*

*Did you know? Mediterranean cuisine stands tall among the finest in the world, celebrated for its vibrant flavors and remarkable health benefits. In 2010, UNESCO honored the Mediterranean diet as an Intangible Cultural Heritage of Humanity. This remarkable diet is characterized by an abundance of fruits, vegetables, whole grains, olive oil, and oily fish, all harmoniously balanced with omega-3 intake. Its minimal reliance on red meat and processed foods plays a vital role in safeguarding against cardiovascular and neurodegenerative diseases.*

The rich variety of ingredients, the wealth of antioxidants, and the plentiful fibers elevate this cuisine to an international benchmark. Research, such as the study published in the New England Journal of Medicine in 2013, validates its remarkable benefits for heart health and the intestinal microbiome.

But the Mediterranean is not merely a single nation: it is a vibrant tapestry of diverse and rich cultures. From Spain to Lebanon, Morocco to Greece, each region contributes its unique flavors and cherished traditions. In this chapter, we will embark on a journey to explore how to elevate the bounty of your Mediterranean garden into a nourishing and sustainable diet.

## 01

# PRECISE ACTIONS, SUCCESSFUL HARVESTS

❋ **Olive harvesting:** gather olives by hand or employ specialized combs to delicately release the fruit into nets positioned beneath the trees. This time-honored technique safeguards the quality of the olives while nurturing the trees.

❋ **Gathering fragrant herbs:** collect them in the early morning, after the dew has settled, to enhance the essential oils of the plants.

❋ **Manual harvest:** hand harvesting enables the selection of the finest bunches, safeguarding the quality of the grapes, often celebrated with vibrant local festivities.

## 02

# TRADITIONAL PRESERVATION METHODS

## SUN DRYING

*Sun drying is a time-honored tradition of the Mediterranean, especially cherished in the sun-drenched regions of Italy, Greece, and Spain. Here, tomatoes, figs, and grapes are lovingly prepared to be preserved in their natural state, free from the constraints of refrigeration.*

Tomatoes, for instance, are halved, gently salted to enhance dehydration, and then arranged on wicker racks or flat surfaces basking in the sun for several days. This technique, cherished in the Mediterranean countryside, preserves not only the vibrant flavors of the produce but also its vital nutrients.

*Drying on racks encourages excellent air circulation and wards off mold. Dried fruits transform into vital components that elevate traditional dishes all year round, allowing the vibrant flavors of summer to shine in winter meals. This method endures as a cherished culinary legacy, lovingly handed down through the ages.*

# PRESERVING OLIVES IN BRINE OR OLIVE OIL

*Preserving olives is a cherished Mediterranean tradition, a practice that has flourished for centuries, allowing these fruits to thrive and their flavors to deepen. The most prevalent technique involves immersing the olives in brine, a solution of salty water, to mellow their inherent bitterness.*

This process is embraced across Italy, Greece, and Spain, where olives are harvested and processed right after picking. Another cherished technique, favored after the olives have been brined, involves preserving them in olive oil, often enhanced with local herbs like rosemary or thyme. This method not only elevates the flavor of the olives but also renders them more supple.

These time-honored traditions ensure a vibrant and genuine flavor that graces Mediterranean cuisines all year round, evoking the warmth of summer even in the depths of winter.

# PASSATA

*The passata technique is a time-honored Italian tradition for preserving tomatoes, especially cherished in the southern regions of Italy, like Campania and Puglia. This beautiful process starts with cooking the tomatoes to tenderize their flesh, followed by passing them through a sieve to extract the skins and seeds.*

This process yields a velvety, concentrated purée. The purée is then sterilized and carefully stored in airtight jars, safeguarding the vibrant flavors of summer for the colder months. Passata represents the mastery of encapsulating the abundance of summer harvests and serves as a fundamental ingredient in numerous classic Italian recipes.

# BOUQUET GARNI

*Crafting bouquets garnis is a time-honored culinary art, rooted in the heart of France yet embraced by numerous Mediterranean cultures. This exquisite technique involves gathering an array of dried aromatic herbs, including thyme, bay leaf, and rosemary, elegantly bound together with string.*

The herbs are gracefully suspended in a dry, well-ventilated space, ensuring that all their remarkable properties are preserved. Once they have dried, these herbs can be utilized in their entirety or ground into a fine powder, adding delightful flavor to soups, stews, or simmered creations. The bouquet garni is gently immersed in dishes during the cooking process, allowing it to subtly infuse its rich flavors, while remaining effortlessly removable before serving. The tradition of using bouquet garni is deeply embedded in Mediterranean culture, where herbs are cherished for their vital role in crafting beloved family recipes.

# 03

# ANCESTRAL PROCESSING METHODS

## THE ART OF NATURALLY FERMENTING VEGETABLES

Lactic fermentation is a remarkable natural process in which bacteria present on vegetables transform sugars into lactic acid, effectively preserving the food.

### ❋ FOR EGGPLANTS AND PEPPERS

- Vegetables are often sliced into delightful chunks or vibrant strips.

- They are then seasoned to draw out excess moisture and encourage fermentation.

- The vegetables find their home in a container, often crafted from glass or ceramic, where they mingle with vinegar, fragrant herbs, and occasionally a drizzle of olive oil.

### FOR COMMONLY USED HERBS AND SPICES

- Garlic, oregano, thyme, bay leaf, and fennel are often embraced to enhance flavor and assist in preservation.

### FERMENTATION TIME

- The journey may span from a handful of days to several weeks, influenced by the recipe and the unique tastes of the community.

### REGIONAL VARIETIES

- In Greece, we discover *toursi*, a delightful array of vegetables transformed through fermentation in vinegar and herbs.
- In Italy, *sottaceti* are vegetables preserved in tangy vinegar, often infused with aromatic herbs.

### BENEFITS

- This approach not only safeguards vegetables but also enhances their digestibility and boosts their probiotic richness.

### USE

- Fermented vegetables frequently grace our tables as antipasti or mezze, beautifully complementing a variety of other dishes.

**In the warmth of summer, we encounter Omar once more.**

From his beautiful garden brimming with tomatoes and herbs, we inquire, *"What will you cook with all of that?"* He shares a list of Syrian dishes, yet we uncover a shared passion for tapenade.

## OMAR'S EXQUISITE TAPENADE

*You will require:*

- *200g of luscious black olives, pitted to perfection.*
- *Two anchovy fillets*
- *1 tablespoon of capers*
- *1 bulb of garlic*
- *3 tablespoons of liquid gold*

1. *In a blender, add the olives, anchovies, capers, and garlic.*
2. *Mix until velvety.*
3. *Slowly incorporate the oil.*
4. *As you blend, gracefully incorporate the olive oil.*
5. *Delightfully serve on toasted bread, chilled to perfection.*

# *At the stone mill,  
the genuine creation of olive oil*

*In the Mediterranean basin, the production of artisanal olive oil transcends mere agricultural technique; it embodies an age-old tradition, a craftsmanship that represents the cultural legacy of an entire region. Traditional mills, known as frantoio in Italy and almazara in Spain, lie at the core of this remarkable process. They employ large stone millstones to crush the olives, often in unison, evoking the communal spirit of the Mediterranean olive grove.*

The journey of creation unfolds through a meticulous ritual: first, the olives are lovingly harvested, often by hand to safeguard their exquisite quality. Next, they are crushed along with their pits beneath grand stone millstones, evolving into a rich paste ready for kneading. The extraction of oil follows, utilizing scourtins—fiber disks—to apply the necessary pressure. While tradition once dictated that oil and vegetation water be separated through decantation, modern producers now embrace centrifuges to enhance this process, all while honoring the essence of their craft.

This artisanal process, often referred to as the first cold pressing, yields an oil of remarkable quality, safeguarding both the fragrances and the nutritional advantages. Yet, in spite of its unparalleled excellence, this time-honored method is less lucrative than contemporary practices. Nevertheless, numerous producers hold steadfast to these techniques, honoring their heritage and tradition.

Beyond production, the crafting of olive oil in these mills becomes a celebration, a moment where the community unites, preserving time-honored traditions in a beautiful exchange of wisdom. Even as the modern world presents new challenges, this practice stands as a vivid testament to the profound connection between humanity, nature, and the rich tapestry of Mediterranean culture.

# PESTO

*Making pesto is a Mediterranean tradition, deeply rooted in the culture of the Genoa region in Italy. While it is commonly paired with pasta, its versatility shines through as it enhances a multitude of dishes, from bruschetta to marinades.*

## INGREDIENTS AND PREPARATION

- **Basil** is the key ingredient, providing a fresh, aromatic flavor.
- **Garlic** is used to enhance the taste of pesto.
- **Pine nuts** add a creamy texture and a slightly sweet taste.
- **Extra virgin olive oil** is essential for the creaminess and richness of the pesto.
- **Parmesan** adds depth of flavor and saltiness.

## TRADITIONAL PREPARATION

- In a mortar (or blender), combine the garlic with coarse salt, crushing it into a rich paste. Next, introduce the basil leaves, continuing to press and release their fragrant essential oils. Add the pine nuts, followed by the finely grated Parmesan cheese. Finally, gradually blend in the olive oil until the mixture is smooth and harmonious.

## 04

# TIMELESS RECIPES TO EMBRACE THE BOUNTY OF YOUR GARDEN

*Your Mediterranean garden is growing with vitality.*

*Fruits, vegetables, and aromatic herbs have finally flourished, presenting a great array of colors and flavors. After a season of dedicated harvesting and preparation, the moment has come to gather around the table. Together, we will embark on a journey through the culinary treasures of the Mediterranean, savoring traditional dishes that honor this bountiful land.*

*From the soul of Greece to the charm of Provence, through the flavors of Italy and Lebanon, every meal draws us nearer to the Mediterranean way of life.*

## *APERITIF*

### GRILLED PEPPER AND OLIVE TAPAS

Let us embark on a delightful journey with an introductory dish, perfect for sharing with friends or family, to be enjoyed without restraint: the beloved traditional Spanish tapas.

Delight in marinated olives and rosemary-roasted peppers, perfectly paired with a refreshing glass of sangria.

*Each region of Spain boasts its own unique tapas specialties. Delight in dishes featuring marinated olives, crispy fried calamari, zesty patatas bravas, or creamy croquettes. The social customs surrounding these culinary treasures are equally varied. The cherished occasion when friends gather in bars to savor tapas is known as tapeo.*

*Tapas can be enjoyed at any hour, yet they hold a special charm in the late afternoon and evening, frequently serving as a delightful prelude to dinner.*

## APPETIZER

### GREEK SALAD

Let's continue with a gentle starter and a colorful Greek salad, mixing cherry tomatoes from your new Mediterranean garden, and garnished with cucumber, onions, feta and fresh basil.

Drizzle everything with olive oil and a squeeze of lemon.

*Greek salad, known as Horiatiki, stands as a vibrant emblem of Mediterranean cuisine, gracing the tables of Greek taverns and restaurants across the globe. It embodies a lifestyle rooted in togetherness, celebrating the joy of sharing meals with loved ones and friends.*

*Enjoyed primarily in the warmth of summer, Greek salad captures the essence of wholesome dining through its vibrant, locally-sourced ingredients.*

## MAIN COURSE

### ZUCCHINI STUFFED WITH RICE AND ROASTED FISH WITH THYME

For the main course, let's dive into the heart of Italy with grilled zucchini stuffed with a fragrant mixture of rice, aromatic herbs and cheese, accompanied by roast fish, delicately seasoned with thyme.

Zucchini from your garden brings a touch of freshness and lightness, while fish offers subtle aromas of thyme.

*The dish Zucchine ripiene con pesce arrosto al timo beautifully captures the essence of simplicity and freshness found in Mediterranean cuisine.*

*The zucchini are carefully hollowed and filled with a delightful rice blend, then roasted alongside a white fish, like hake, gently infused with thyme. This union of vegetables and fish beautifully emphasizes the harmony of flavor and lightness, while celebrating the bounty of the garden. An ideal creation for wholesome, inviting cooking, brimming with natural fragrances.*

## SIDE

### BREAD TABOUNA

To accompany the main course, we suggest you try the Tunisian tabouna bread, perfectly cooked in a traditional oven.

The mixture of aromatic herbs from the garden with the soft texture of the bread creates a perfect harmony of flavors, recalling the authenticity of Mediterranean meals shared with family or friends.

*Tabouna bread stands as a testament to the rich tapestry of Tunisian cuisine, steeped in a tradition that spans millennia. Baked in a clay oven that shares its name, it captures the essence of Mediterranean simplicity and authenticity. Crafted from flour and semolina, often adorned with fennel seeds, it is lovingly kneaded by hand to achieve a delightful elasticity, then transformed into flat pancakes through the baking process. This cherished moment of preparation, shared among family, weaves connections and sustains the legacy of culinary traditions.*

*Today, tabouna stands as a link to Tunisia, reaching out to those who may be distant from its shores.*

# DESSERT

## PROVENÇAL FIG TART

Let's conclude with a sweet note, thanks to the delicious Provençal tart with fresh figs, topped with honey and sprinkled with crunchy nuts.

This dessert celebrates the sweetness of seasonal fruits, enhanced by the rich texture of nuts and the deliciousness of local honey, for a light end to a meal.

*Provençal fig tart stands as a beloved dessert from the enchanting South of France, honoring the exquisite fresh figs, a quintessential Mediterranean delight. This delightful tart is traditionally crafted on a foundation of shortcrust or sablé pastry, adorned with a luscious blend of almond powder and fig jam. The figs, elegantly quartered, are artfully arranged in a rosette and baked to perfection in the oven until they reach a tender, melt-in-your-mouth softness.*

*This dessert beautifully captures the essence of local ingredients, creating a delightful balance of crunchy and soft, sweet and subtly tangy.*

## TEA

### MOROCCAN MINT TEA

To conclude this Mediterranean meal in style, head to your garden to pick a few fresh Moroccan mint leaves. Prepare a traditional mint tea, a symbol of hospitality in Morocco, to delicately accompany the sweetness of the fig tart.

The intoxicating scent of infused mint, combined with a touch of sugar, creates a refreshing drink that balances the sweet flavors of the dessert.

*Moroccan mint tea, though introduced in the 19th century, has blossomed into a powerful cultural emblem of warmth and hospitality in Morocco. Its emergence, linked to English traders in search of new markets, swiftly gave rise to a distinctive fusion of green tea and vibrant local mint.*

*Crafted through a cherished ritual, it is presented in three consecutive glasses, each one sweeter than the last. This tea, enjoyed during family gatherings or among friends, symbolizes generosity and reverence in Moroccan culture.*

# IN CLOSING

As we approach the conclusion of this Mediterranean adventure, we trust that it has been both delightful and uplifting. This guide has equipped you with the tools to craft your own sanctuary of freshness, tranquility, and warmth, so cherished by Mediterranean traditions.

If you reside in the north, let us remember that climate change is increasingly evident, demanding greater resilience and the sharing of knowledge and wisdom between our region and beyond. Yet, the flow of knowledge and cultural practices is not a novel concept: take the tomato, for instance, which hails from the Andean regions and made its way to the Mediterranean in the 16th century, brought back from America by the Spanish. With its remarkable adaptability, it has flourished to become a vital component in numerous cuisines, including those of the northern nations.

So, perhaps the Mediterranean garden, with its remarkable ability to withstand drought and its deep bond with water systems, will become the essential choice of tomorrow, no matter where you are. Embrace it and allow yourself to be enchanted by the wonder of this eternal journey!

# AN EXCLUSIVE
## *gift*
### IS WAITING JUST FOR YOU

Ready to continue the journey?
Scan here!

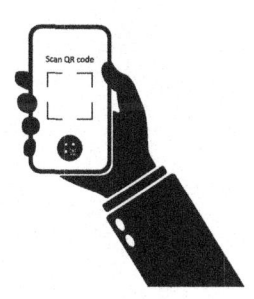

# BY THE SAME AUTHOR

- *Create Your Tibetan Garden:*
  *Tibetan Ancestral Knowledge*

- *Protect Your Garden Without Chemicals*
  *Mauritian Traditional Knowledge*

- *Herbarium Of America*
  *From the Northeast to the Mid-Atlantic*

- *Gardening with the Moon around the World*
  *Ancestral Farming Knowledge*

- *Relieve Menstrual Pain With Herbal Remedies*
  *Ancestral Healing Knowledge of Women*

- *Cultivating During Wartime*
  *Knowledge and Resilience of the World*

Original title :
*Grow Your Mediterranean Garden In The City: Ancestral Wisdom Of The Seas*

© 2024, Vergers du Monde

All rights reserved.
No part of this guide may be copied, reproduced, or distributed without prior permission from the publisher.

Authored by Hélène Bourry, as a writer for Vergers du Monde.
Collection : World Agricultural Knowledge
Book Collection Number : 7

## DON'T MISS OUR NEXT PRACTICAL GUIDES!

Join our newsletter for monthly agricultural insights.

## VISIT US ONLINE

▶ vergersdumonde

📷 vergersdumonde

www.vergersdumonde.org

Made in the USA
Las Vegas, NV
21 December 2024